Spectrum

Annette D. Pateman

Pateran Press

Pateran Press
UK
Canada

ISBN 978-0-46-450498-6

First edition

Cover Photograph by John Pateman
Author Photograph by Saskia Pateman

www.worditry.com

Acknowledgements

Thank you to my husband John who encouraged me to publish my writing.

*Thank you to my children
Lianne, Joe and Saskia who encourage me, always.*

Thank you to Margaret Demillo whose intelligence and creativity gave form to this book.

Dear Readers,

I write poems that are concerned with issues of identity, diaspora and relationships.

My poems seek to take you on a journey and allow you to glimpse the world through my eyes.

Annette Pateman

Table of Contents

Ants Will Come
Jamaican Patois

If you do wrong,
      ants
will come a me grave
      an tell me

Black People

We bring the warmth of the sun.
The heartbeat of the talking drum.
We hear it in our music.
R n B, blues, jazz, hip- hop and reggae.
Soca, hi-life and calypso.
The rhythms of Africa,
Spread through the black diaspora.
We are beautiful.
Strong beyond measure.
Used to build cities and nations.
Brick by brick.
Stone by stone.
Many are the wrongs done,
For which they don't atone.
We find joy in life.
We find joy in the day.
Black History Month.
Hooray!

I am from

I am from my mother's belly,
my Black mother's belly.
My father's heart
my forefathers' blood.
I am from the Black and the white

The fire and the ice.
The hot fire and the melt.
As one, as one, as many.
I am from out of many,
one people.

The hot and the cold.
I am from the blood stain.
I am from the perspiration,
pant and the shiver.
I am from the scream.
I am from the earth.
I am from the sun.

I am from the gentle breeze
bristling across my neck.

I am from air.
I am from water,
tip tap tip tap.
I am from deep
dark laughter
in the night

I am from the strangled sob
I am from
everywhere.

Skin

"You are not too dark".
"Not too light".
Said a friend who thought it was a lark,
to comment on my skin.
As though it were a coat to put on and take
off.
But of course I won't.

"You are not too dark".
"Not too light"
Said a friend who thought it was a joke to
comment on my coat

Made me feel it was a sin
to wear the skin that I am in.
It's my yoke.
It's not a joke.

Hair

Oil, twist,
part, plait.
This is my hair
and how I do that.

I smooth on the oil.
I hold to the hair.
I take my comb
and make partings with care.

The strands in my hand
I move and position.
I weave and discover
Creation my mission.

Now is the time to
acknowledge the scalp.
Stroke and knead
make the style to suit.

This is my hair,
Afro, frizzy, dread and locs.
Yes, this is the crown
I wear in town.

Blackness

Blackness is the other.
Dark skin and often
coiled, kinky hair.
It is the look and sometimes,
the stare.

People gather and utter!
But none want to be the other.
Blackness is strange fruit
hanging from the tree.

Blackness is dusky limbs
Smoothness, secret dark.
It is the joy that comes
when we dance in the dark.

Blackness is when two or
more are gathered,
we feel undone.
It represents trouble,
but we seek none.

Blackness is the cradle of all life.
Before, at the beginning, the seed.
Then comes the fear and the strife.

Blackness is the hand reach out to touch.
The scared look, bad comment,
even in a sacred place.

Blackness is triumph.
After all we are still here.
Even though none would want to wear
our skin or our hair.

My Mother White

My mother White
My father Black
There is nothing
Wrong with that.

Two people in love
Brought forth my life.
I came into a world
That is rife with strife.

I am not Black.
I am not White either.
I am between.
That makes me keener.

To make others see
that life is neither,
Black, White,
Yellow, Brown or Red

I want to put to bed
the feel of your dread,
at my being in the world
rejection unsound.

Let me be,
then you will see.
All the beauty that is in me.

I will weave and create.
I will inspire and love.
I will flower and reach tall
and not grow to hate.

The Black and the White

The Black and the White
The servant, the master.
The master, the servant.
Will it be forever thus.
You and I.
I and you.
Made for each other.
There was no clue.

When my eyes close in
the endless sleep.
I would (like) the world
(to) know that I crossed
the street and (crossed)
the wide maw to know
you and take you as
my lover.

I Black.
I dreamed that we held hands
and touched cheeks in a crowded
(place) and none looked or stared.
We walked, (we lived) we loved.
We argued.
In short we lived and
No one moaned.

Black Indian

What is it to be a Black Indian?
To hear the sound of the drum and to
know the rhythm of the earth,
in the heart.

To hold the thick braids,
whose tight curls tell the truth to the fingers.
To carry the bloodline of a tribe and a nation.
Long lost to the present situation.

What is it to be the last of your kind
the one who knows the last songs,
the last words of the language?
What is it to be the one who learns through a DNA test,
that shows the one per cent Native American.
Whose long lost and almost silenced ancestor, calls out
through the blood and DNA.

"I am here."
" I lived."
 "I loved."
"I walked the same earth as you."
" I drank from the same river."
"My hair was long and black."
"My eyelashes were straight and dark,
 like yours."
" Can't you see you?"
" Can't you see me?"

What is it to be Black Indian?
It is to be me.

A person of African ancestry,
whose antecedents were taken in misery.
From that great continent Africa.
The cradle of life and our birth.
Far away across the sea,
to a land called Jamaica.
Situated in the Caribbean Sea.
Named after the Carib Indians,
who were the Indigenous people there.
And in that place, your bloodline linked with mine.
And you hoped that through the African people,
your life would survive.

And so I am a Black Indian.

Taino Dreams

Today was as hard as chiseled glass.
Yesterday was bright and soft as candy floss.
Red riding hood carried her basket happily in the
beginning
Sleeping beauty slept through it all.
Today cut through the image of mother
calling and welcoming. Soft arms outstretched.
The Taino people welcomed Christopher Columbus
and now they are no more.
They left behind the gift of the hammock
that swings to and fro
and brings dreams and sleep.
The virgin stands as still as stone.
Arms outstretched, atop the water fountain.
There found buried in the ground.
Rough grey stone carving of a
goddess named Atabey.
She too likes water and rivers and lakes.
Taino worship of her was profound.
Sleep and time. Time and sleep.
Then there is the forgetting.
Round and around.

The Creole

These are the now forbidden words that described
Black persons.
>   *Mulatta*, half Black.
>   *Quadroon*, quarter Black.
>   *Octroon*, one eighth Black.

We know that many were the deals,
that money crossed palms at houses,
for access to the women that possessed the
quantum that denoted
that they were
>   *Mulatta*
>   *Quadroon*
>   *Octroon*
 A lighter shade of Black.
Sometimes creole, and sometimes just light skin Black.

In the time of transatlantic slavery.
All kinds of chicanery.
The buying and selling of lives.
The buying and selling of
liberty.

A special kind of purchase,
that is rooted in the baser instinct.

The creole bore her gift
and her burden.
A lighter shade of person.
Growing on the master's
plantation.

Yes I am Black

Yes I am Black.
What is wrong with that?
Some say ni
I am not a forgiver.

Yes I am Black.
What is wrong with that?
Some say we are lawless
and lazy.
I say you are definitely crazy!

After all did we not pick cotton in the field,
sun up to sun down
and keep the plantation home
so even now
they are found beautiful, expensive and proud.

Yes I am Black.
What is wrong with that?
Are you curious to know
what it is like to be that?
Is that the fact that takes you aback?

Yes I am Black
and I wouldn't change that.
I have lived with myself
in my skin
for the whole of my life
and wouldn't change this
after the fact.

Yes I am Black.
what is wrong with that?
I suggest you grow up
and understand that the world
Is like that.

We are varied and different,
a beautiful creation.

The Other

What do you see
When you look upon me?
A person Black or Brown
and unlike thee.

I am the other.
Described by my skin.
A Black woman.
A Brown woman.
Never your kin.

I live on the other side of town,
and sometimes you see me around.
Why are you here? How did you begin?
These are the questions you ask my kin.

My body a statement.
My hair its crown.
I am the one
you don't want around.

If you gave me a chance,
you might get to know.
And then you would see,
the person that's me.

But for now I remain the Other.
My back made to suffer,
the whispers and slurs
and looks and wonder.

Hide

What is the cost when we hide our identity
Strong woman
Strong man
Black Woman
Black man
Does hiding come at the cost of our
Integrity

What does it cost you to hide your identity
In the outward show of skin or culture or clothing

The cost is dis-ease
Fear,
Anxiety.
A kind of self loathing.

The cost of
just passing.
Blending in.
Being accepted.
But not really.
Because,
you know
the truth.

And so you listen to the sound of your heart
and turn down the beats that remind you,
of the start.
When you were just you
and not a part;
of a society that has the power
to set you apart.

Racism

Racism is bred from
Fear and loathing.
The cut of words on the skin.
The taint and the hating.

The father is fear
The mother is loathing.
All the while
Ignorance is the fetid air,
that feeds the disclosing.

Racism
Is the power to
Cast the other out.
Like Cain
so that true peace
Is forever without.

The Gatekeeper

You are the gatekeeper.
You control the flow.
You open the gate,
for those you know.

The people you know
look and speak like you.
They come walk through
with the privilege they own.

I am the outsider,
Unknown to you.
You will close the gate,
to keep those like you.

You are the gatekeeper.
What can I do
To cause you to open
To someone different too you?

Slave

I am not slave.
I was enslaved.
I am not slave.
I was enslaved.

I walked free in the sun,
In the land of my birth.
Baobab tree,
Sheltered me.
Yam and banana
Fed me.
My family around me
Grew me.
My beloved,
Loved me.
Until you came and took me.
Away across the sea.
To a land of plantations.
Where there is only memory of
What was and can never again be.

I am not slave.
I was enslaved.
I am not slave
I was enslaved.

 There is a refrain in this poem.
This can be repeated by the audience and listener.

Race Science

What is this race science
Is it the study of differences
between races of people.
Or is it the study of difference
so as to divide.

What is race?
It is a man made construct.
Forged from the fires of division
and then hate.
So we are left in a
divided state.

Waiting at the gate.

Office

Today my boss called me into the office
You are the one that ticks all the boxes.
You are Black, female, disabled,
Now I feel enabled

I am the worker that is an enabler.
The person who makes my boss Liberator.
Because I am Black, female and disabled.
In a tick box world,
I am required material.

Photograph

The photograph shows memory reflected in
black and white
and shades of grey.
Just like my memories.
The photo is there but an unreal reflection
of something that really was.

Memory like shifting shades on a page
Faded into sepia shades.

Sometimes there is a splash of colour
a bright yellow or green or sky blue.
Just enough to reassure that this is real.
That day I stood on the shore.

Memory like a black and white photo
caught up in the pages of age.
It was real to me.
Now mere black and white and sepia shades

Wanting You

Wanting you
   An ache
 In my belly
  A gnawing
In the soul of me
   Creeping weakness
In my legs

Doth Thou Love Me True?

I put my hand
in thine,
and thought that
you were mine.
Doth thou love me
true?
If only I knew.

Loves You More

I am the one who loves you more,
who stands at the gate and
waits by the door.

I watch for your smile
the dimple arrives,
but none but me would keep the score.

There exists a 'she' between our past,
our future, present
perhaps till the last.

I wish that I could change
my fate,
from the one that came too late.
For she had already taken your heart,
and held on to it,
never to part.

I am the one who waits by the gate,
resigned and accepting,
I swallow my fate.

You Don't See Me

You look at me,
Yet you don't see me.
You touch me,
But you don't feel me.
You hear me,
 but you don't listen me.

Hold Your Head

I saw you hold your head
        and hunch your
shoulder.

I know that you no longer
        love her.

But too late to turn back,
        for fear of,
renting her asunder.

Fair Haired Maiden

The memory of a fair head maiden
has oft wandered with me.
Tearing down the walls of my soul.
Etching away the peace of my mind

Oft doth the memory of you assail me.
Appearing like the morning dew,
on a rosebud in the faint spring sunshine.

Although I would that the memory of you
leave me.
I know I would lament the loss.
For thou art a part of me.

Loon Song

The loon sits high in the tree
Singing
Lonely me
My mate
Come and find me

Loon sits high in the tree
Singing
Maybe it's my time
Mate come and find me

Loon sits high in the tree
There beside him
Sits his family
Singing

Loon Song
Loon song
Come hear my
Loon Song
Soon
I will be gone

A Question about Hair Dye

When we dye our hair
and cover our roots.
Are we searching
for eternal youth?

My Beauty

Blurring my eyes,
blurred lines.
My beauty slipping away
from me.

My beauty,
that minx
in the red coat.

That gorgeous young
woman with the smiling mouth.
That female with the lustrous
and flashing eyes.

Don't leave me today.
Stay with me a while longer.

Lake Day

Today is a day for joy.
Water splashing.
The air is humming and the camera clicking.
Trying to capture the heart of the day.

A granddaughter floating in her pink blow up boat.
This is the first time.
A grandson with a fistful of sand
Testing the water.
A beautiful teenage granddaughter,
Swimming in bright red lipstick.
Hindu, gold, Shiva medallion,
 around her neck.

Water

What is underneath the water.
I sense a torrent moving.
Almost sinuously.
with no regard
for........things

The Forgotten Poem

I am the forgotten poem
who sits in the drawer.
Sometimes when a breeze blows,
I flutter to the floor.

I am the forgotten poem
who listens for the door,
that signals the return of my Maker.
The hinge and the floor.

I am the forgotten poem
now silenced but not silent.
The marks on my pages growing fainter,
but not gone.

I am the forgotten poem
my voice loud and clear
Hear me and read me,
just let me be here.

I am the forgotten poem,
Swirls and whorls make up my body.
The words stoppered by your hand.
And memory.

I am the forgotten poem,
left lying and at rest.
Waiting for the time when my voice sounds
from your breast.

I am the forgotten poem
who sits in the drawer.
The clasp of the lid,
the hinge of the door.

I am the forgotten poem.
My time is hear.
You will listen me now.
No longer future year.

I am the forgotten poem,
your hand grazed me today.
You selected a letter,
then went on your way.

I am the forgotten poem.
Forgotten no more.
My voice rings out loud and clear,
timbre strong and true.

I am the forgotten poem.
My power is profound.
I will move you and mark you,
In ways not yet found.

I am the forgotten poem.
But forgotten no more.
I am come into being,
with a ferocious roar.

Tomorrow

I welcome you.
Yet fear you still.
Will you bring wholesome gifts,
of love, plenty and beauty to my life?
Or will you gift me with
sorrow, anxiety and want.

Dear tomorrow the egg
cracks,
and life flows,
tomorrow.
The good, the bad,
 the beautiful and the ugly.
All coalesce to make,
tomorrow.

Mango

He hands me a ripe mango
He smiles shyly as he offers it to me.
I take it and look at it.
I notice this mango has brown skin.
Darker than mine.
He is waiting.
Waiting for me to bite into this sweet gift.
I bite and gold yellow mango juice
runs down my chin.
Sublime on my tongue.

Thank you Devon
I say to my cousin when I have wiped
My mouth with the back of my hand.

Basket

I lean over the riverbank,
a dull ache gathers in the small of my back,
Reminding me that I have been in this space,
everyday this week.

I soak and beat the green palm fronds
and the water shines silver against my brown arms.
I lay out the fronds to dry flat, on a white cotton sheet.

Then I begin to weave a basket, bag or a maybe a hat
My hands and my heart will decide that.

The baskets contain my dreams and some tears,
of foreign lands, a new life, a home and no fears.

I sell the baskets for three pennies a piece.
Upon this foundation,
I build hope for better times.

The Letter

I waited by the banana tree,
where you first saw me.
I shaded sun under the leaves.
Watched as others got letters
from foreign.

Saw the faces crack brilliant smiles.
Hands grasping paper
that meant they were going.
 Bodies gyrating with joy.

I waited by the banana tree
where you first saw me.
Wondering why your letter
did not find me.

Was the one you called more special than me
was she more cultured?
More beautiful?
Was her skin softer than mine?
Was she more woman than me?

The answers never came.
You never explained.
I waited by the banana tree,
where you first saw me.

As she sauntered pass me unknowing,
her body freely swaying.
Going to the market,
to buy things for foreign.

Lost and found Quartz

Swing and twirl.
Catching the light and the fireflies,
light as air,
Travelling.
My quartz sparkles and lives in the sun.
I move smooth as a bird.

Now is the Time of the Bear Hunt

(to be read with a galloping rhythm)

Now is the time of the bear hunt.
Now is the time of the bear hunt.
To shoot and to kill
the joy and the thrill.
Now is the time of the bear hunt.

Now is the time of the bear hunt.
Now is the time of the bear hunt.
The gun and the dagger.
The spear and the arrow.
Now is the time of the bear hunt.

Now is the time of the bear hunt.
(grunt, grunt)
Now is the time of the bear hunt.
(drum, drum)
Time to leave the fear
and gather and cheer.
Now is the time of the bear hunt.

Three Women

Three women sit in a hotel room.
Sharing.

One sits at the hotel table looking at the
messages on her mobile phone.
Swiping.

One sits on her bed,
phone propped up on her knees.
Playing scrabble.

The other sits on the hotel issued armchair,
writing this observation,
called a poem.

Picture this,
three women from a book group.
The white grey light of early winter coming
filtered through the hotel issue net curtain.

What will happen next is uncertain.

Perhaps some conversation,
taking up the earlier discussion of metaphor.
Perhaps a sojourn to the winter film festival.
Perhaps a meal and
then a walk to the winter festival bonfire.

Three women.
Two white,
one black.
In a hotel bedroom.

The human fish dives
deep into the ice cold water.
Her body sheathed in black rubber.
Bubbles of air issue from her lips and nose as she nudges
the ceiling of ice with her face.
In this world all is still silence and she experiences
grace in that quiet space.

The screen flickers as she exits
the blue grey water, through the
self made hole in the ice- in Finland.
The credits roll.
The fire pit sheds it's heat and warmth,
to human hands stretched forth to reach that
radiant heat.
And shards
of fire motes dance and drift around.
There are smiles and laughter and a black dog
called Luke lets me stroke his head and his ear.

One woman leads the way to the car and the food,
that awaits in a place filled with people and a curved bar,
and a waitress with blonde pigtails.
The other woman orders Walleye and mashed potato,
when we all sit down.
The other chooses a stew fit for fishermen, with salmon,
that comes tardy but tasty.

The three women talk of,
the games people play...

including the complex game called Bridge.
Then there is red wine and a hot tub that is
a revelation.
Then quiet in the bedroom,
a kind of evening meditation.

Three women.
Two white
and one black.

There is a Vortex Coming

There is a vortex coming and
I want to be at its centre.
For its centre is still and quiet and
 a place where things can be created.
Further out there is the wind.
A fighting movement, and it isn't possible
 to stand upright and think and create.
So I know there is a vortex coming
and I want to stand at its heart where
there is stillness and silence and space
to create.

The Tales of the Good

The tales of the good,
so rarely get told.
The tales of the good,
lost in the fold of the
pages of a book.

You welcomed me and smiled.

Come and sit with me a while,
tis late and you have hurried
 o pass this way.

You gave me coffee and good cheer.
A Tim Horton's was near and
you showed me the way.
You knit me a toque,
and gave me a look that
said
You are welcome
to stay.

Little Black Choirboy

Little Black choirboy
you truly sing like a lark.
None but us could tell your
Voice apart from the
White voices in the choir group at church.

Not many people knew that you had
a pure descant voice.
A true soprano.
Prized by choirmasters far and wide.

That you walked behind the priests and their helpers.
To take your place on the raised dais,
that held the choir that much closer to God,
the creator.

A wonderful thing for us to see.
A favour for our brother.
The little Black choirboy.

The Gate

I am the gate.

                    Through me comes

the next generation.

                    For that I deserve

honour and

                    appreciation.

I am woman.

Easter Goddess

Goddess seated in the spring sun.
Black skin gleaming.
A wave of her hand, butterfly wings flutter.
A whisper of wind against the tree trunk.
Spring has sprung.
Roots push hard, white fingers against dark brown soil.
The red speckled egg trembles in the downy nest.
Soft feathers line this wooden cradle of tree branches.
The egg coalesces into true clear life.
Cosmic egg.
Mythical egg.
Easter egg.
Oh hail and hear the names of the ancient ones.
Ishtar, Eostra, Isis, Freya, Oshun, Yemaya, Aphrodite,
Kali
Feminine energy of life and growth.
Let us dance and hold hands and rejoice.
Spring is here sprung.
Easter is here.
Happy Easter everyone.

The Favourite

For the longest time
I thought I was adopted.
But then it turned out,
I was actually allotted.
The place behind my sister,
'The favourite'

Sister

Sister I always loved you
more than you loved me.
Even when a gift was brought
for you from overseas.
You gave it to me,
for the giver brought no gift for me.

Sister I always loved you
more than you loved me.
This became clear when you
gained power over me.

The Will was written.
You were the head.
Sister you thought of you, yourself
your children, and left me for dead.

Sister I always loved you
more than you loved me.
Remember the sharing of clothes,
dancing, cosmetics and bags.
I never really understood bags but you
always showed me.

Sister I still love you more
than you love me.
I wish for a time when we can be free,
of life's inequities and woes.
That separated you internally from me.

Missing Brother

When the message came through that you were
missing.
I didn't believe it.
 A day passed, and I still didn't believe it
Another day passed, and still I didn't believe it
Until a week passed, and I couldn't believe it.

My brother where are you?
Are you in a place happy, looked after,
Safe and sound.
Or has someone hurt you,
Taken advantage of your clear heart.
Gentle mind.

You are the kindest of brothers.
Your life potential damaged as you were,
being born.
And so you lived without a partner
Without someone to hold.
You, who are the the most giving of us all.

Where are you brother?
Come home
Please come home.
We will visit you and see you more often.
And work to make your life more whole.

I love you brother.
I remember good, past,
young times.
Come home.
Missing brother.

Brother

How is it possible to know
a brother, who died before I was
even born.

And yet,
I do know you brother.
I hear your laugh.
A soft chuckle which
makes dimples and then
It's gone.

Your voice a quiet rain.
Your movements,
smooth and precise.
A quiet gentle person.
Thoughtful.

Isn't this why people
love you?

My uncle who is almost
the last of my mother's
generation,
talks about you still.

Even in this conversation on his
birthday,
he talks to me about you.

You are loved still,
brother.
I know you.

A person of balanced feature and form.
I know you even though you died before
I was even born.

You were a person who listened well,
and loved his mother.
A person who was dutiful.
That most old fashioned of words.
Which is big and loud in meaning
yet deep and quiet with action.

I also love you brother.
Even though you died before
I was born.

Written for my brother Glen.
Glendell Howell Lawrence

Respect Brother

Respect brother
Respect brother
This is the old greeting.
The old way of seeing.
The old way of acknowledging.
One to the other.
It is at the centre of things.
Respect, the thing that was taken.
The thing that was assaulted.
But we try to reclaim it,
when we greet each other.
With the word.
Respect

Respect 2

With this word
We see each other
And gift each other
with the gift of respect.
We convey it onto one another
And shower each other with the idea
and the gift of
respect

Respect 3- Meanings

I see you.
I acknowledge you.
I wish you well.
I wish you well now,
In this moment.
I give you respect
I give you respect now in this moment
You are worthy of respect as a human being.
You are worthy of respect.
I respect you.

Happy

What is it be happy?

Is it to count the hours
Of the office day?

Is it to sit around a fire,
with friends and family?

Is it to count the white goods
in the shopping trolley?

Or take a coconut from a tree?
Is it all about the *money*?

Tanning Lady

She lays on the
tanning bed.
The rays from the
glass tubes
glow,
as they
toast her.
Just so.
Until she is just the
right colour
of brown......

She lays there.
A white eye mask
covers her eyes.
Protecting them
from the rays that
come from
the long glass
tubes.

The electromagnetic
rays,
darken her skin.
Just so.
Afterwards she exits the
clam shell space that is
the tanning bed
and dons a
Fluffy white
dressing gown...

Surprise

Surprise is when a person
   wakes from a long
slumber
   and realizes that it is spring
and will soon be
   summer.

The time is now.
   Beginnings will flow.
Flowers will bloom
   and trees will blossom.

The caterpillar will wake
   from its pupae sleep
and we will see a butterfly
   that we can't keep.

This is surprise.
   Rejoice and wake
refreshed.

   Life is surprise!!

Stare

Today I walked into a room
   I was the only Black person there.
      The only Black person for miles around
         The eyes were on me
            Many chose to
               stare....

Noah's Ark

We float here.
On a kind of
Noah's ark.
A boat that will
Take us all.
Jamaican, Trinidadian
Ghanaian and South African.
and many from the continent
and the Greater and Lesser Antilles.
But one thing sets us apart.
We are black people.
That time when we would
walk apart from one another,
Is gone forever.
For the world sees not
the different countries of
Africa and America and the Islands of the Caribbean
It sees the black and brown and sometimes
white that makes us black people.
So we float here,
On a kind of Noah's ark.
A boat that will take us all,
and that cannot tell us apart.

Giver of Breath and Souls

You who are the giver of breath and souls.
　　Who has looked upon me and
　　　now my children are,
　　　　no more.

You are the one that thunders.
　The rainbow in the sky.
　　You are the one that lights fires.

You are the giver of rain.
　We see you in the sunshine.
　You are without limit.

　　　Thus,
　you are everywhere.

Fish Dance

The American white pelican
floats lightly on Lake Superior.

The pelican plucks fish
From the lake.
It's beak bulging with Pisces.
The seagulls look on
and wait for the moment
that a fish falls from the beak pouch
and so the fish dance begins.

With a swoop and excited
bird calls, they catch the falling fish
and fill their own seagull bellies.
Feasting at the fish dance
A dance of life and death.

Cord

My grandmother buried
the navel.
       The baby cord.
 The strength that connected me
 to my baby.
       She buried it under,
tree root.
 The sacred part of
       my baby.

The tree would take
 the strength back into,
       its body.

Breathe the air,
 and eat the earth.
       That was once a part,
 of my body,

Polygamist

I am the second wife.
I live in the house and scrub the floor.
But when the first wife is out,
 you shut the door,
I am the second wife and more.

 You fall on my breast
and tumble me on the floor.
I have no real station,
 the first wife is at the door.

Call me by my first name,
slave no more.

Today Is Your Last Day

Today is your last day
Death will come without a gown.
Today is your last day
death will take you without a sound.

Today is your last day
If only you knew.
What would you say?
What would you do?

Today is the last day
tomorrow never turning.
The dew on your brow,
The sun in the morning.

Today is your last day,
the bright of my smile.
Today is your last day,
"Please death wait a while"

Anansi

Anansi, you fancy yourself
part spider
part man
Part God

Created from the breath of the Akan in Ghana.
Passed on through sweat and toil and sugar by
the enslaved Africans in Jamaica.

Anansi, you egg eater
and heart breaker.
A trickster who can follow
the eagle to reach the domain of the sky God.

Anansi, keeper of dark wisdom
and magic.
You traverse parallel worlds
to complete your journey.

You force us to face the shadow in the corner.
The knock at the door in the darkest night.

The fear that lives within us all.
You uncover, and you cause us to discover,
the ability to conquer,
the unknowable and overwhelming.
The scary and the frightening.

Anansi spider man.
Your web is full of holes.
Made up of the strings that make up this
Uni(verse)

I
The daughter of an Akan ancestor,
salute you.

Dreadlocs

Baby Locs
My baby locs coil
black and soft,
Like ringlets lying
gentle against my head.
They are new and vulnerable.

A silk scarf which
encircles my crown at night
protects them from the movement
of my head against the pillow

Teen Locs
My locs start to
bud and grow,
and a new form is born.

My hair curling
and coiling until
the strands become
so close that a loc bud,
is made.

The loc bud
elongates and begins
to grow upward and downward.

Till a new loc
 is made and a
loc is formed.

A teen loc.
New and wayward.
Springy and full
of life.

(continued)

Not easy to train.
A challenge to style
yet beautiful.

Adult Locs
My locs now fully formed
and confident.
They grow like fresh shoots
and now I can really see the length
and the time spent to get to this space.

Loc love
is what I experience as
I get to know my locs.

Elder Locs
These elder locs of mine have seen life.
They are made of strands of,
joy, happiness and being glad.
Sadness too is intertwined.
They are sage with wisdom and knowledge.

Sometimes heavy and long
against my head, neck and back.
I wrap them in bright cloth,
with which I protect and lift them.
A form of antigravity.

Often I let them be free and open.
They love the fresh air and to move gently,
When the wind blows.

Locs an expression of
resistance, essence and strength.
Coiling and spiralling,
Like my DNA.

My locs.
An organic antenna
Reaching into the world.
My locs an outward
expression of my soul.

Sometimes I adorn them
with natural metal
and crystal and shell.

Elder locs curling and fully formed,
a protection and grace is their gift to me.

Formed from my DNA.
An outward extension of life.
A spiral eternity.

Blood Memory

My blood runs with memory,
that sings and soars inside
with words like heat and love,
hurt and pain.

For what had the master to gain?

Blood memory.
In the throat.
Bubbling up from the chest.

I will do my best
to help you to rest peacefully.

Fireflies wink not in bottles
but against a black sheet sky,
with white pin point lights that
glitter and blink.

I ask why, why me?
Is it because my skin is fair and
white like she?
Is it because my waist is small
and tight?

Is it because I am octoroon?
My great grandmother an African woman,
who knew African heat and land but could not speak
the words.
Only toil and work the land.

Pepper Pot Soup

Mouth lowers to the
spoon and sips at the soup.
Tongue tastes the yam and
starchy white dasheen.
The scent of fresh thyme
hovers above the pot.
An aroma that evokes
memories of Jamaican mother.
The green finger like
shape of okra.
A ladies finger.
Makes a gentle curve
in the liquid.
Spoon dips to catch
Okra, and a red piece of
scotch bonnet floats by.
Spicy warmth follows
where pepper soup
is fed.

She

She who did not see
the beauty that
was within her
and without her, grace.
Whose eyes were blinded
to the beauty of her
cheek, and the bones
that made up
her face.

The grace of her fingers,
that could produce
a tasty and bounteous feast.

The touch of her hand on
a brow that could
bring peace.

She could not see,
because her corner was dark
and darkness was in the face of her heart.

She who loved
and cared for others
but could not find
or see her own worth.

Book

Book is not just paper and marks on a page.
Book is glue and ink
sometimes leather and thread.

Book is a story to take to bed.
A comfort in the night, when alone in bed.

Book can be words of beauty,
or words of dread.

Book is the memory of youth and sometimes
a memoir that ends in dead.

Book is history and future tomorrow.
Book is looking back into the dark night.

Book is technology and space.
Book is the myriad tongues of the human race

Book the elixir of life.
Book brings meaning to our lives.

I Chose to Fly Away

I chose to fly away
when the world of the then squeezed
me too tight and shut out the light and the hope that
that gave my life meaning.

It was then that I flew and left
the Isles of my birth and came to a place
where a Sleeping Giant lay
hands crossed over his breast.

In that place
I found the breath of creation
that caught like a spark and gave me the courage to
sing as
a lark sings.

Memory Going

I can feel the memory.
There on the edge.

I can taste the memory.
There just behind the mirror.

I can see the memory.
There just beyond the
blue sky.

I can sense the memory.
There, just slipping away
from me.

The Girls by the Water Fountain

You know them.
The girls by the water fountain.
They go there to talk and chat
about.....others.

About what is happening,
in their lives but mostly in the
lives of others.

They have a leader.
She is the prettiest of them all.
The one with the information,
the latest news,
a clarion call.

Then there is me.
Watching the show from the sidelines.
Through the sides of my eyes I catch the
whispers and lowered eyes.

I am sent to Coventry.
A place where there is no fountain.
In Coventry there is no pretty leader.
Just me with my integrity.
Some would say it is lonely.
I say it is a place like a hide.
I can see the girls by the fountain as if,
they were in a slide show.

One by one the images flow.
Then the pictures sit side by side.
An unending tide.

Yet I am here still in Coventry.
I am not washed away.
I am not faded.
I am just excluded from the circle.
They are the girls by the water fountain.
With that I am okay.

Left

I am the one that
is left on the tree.
The one with the bruise on the skin
that they choose not to see.

I am the one that is
left on the tree.
Hands touch and stroke
and then pass by me.

I am the one that is
left on the tree.
Round and full
and ready to be plucked.

I am the one that falls
to the ground.
I roll and stumble
and bounce around.

I am the one
that sought out fertile soil.
Whose roots scrambled,
for dew drops and water.

I am the tree that
holds up the
fruit, that others
look at and pick over.

Dark Haired Maiden

A dark haired maiden
Whose tresses lie against her
Back like smooth dark silk
You carry a soft warm heart
The empathy and love you
give sets you far apart
From others who would
if they had the chance
tear you apart

Stand unbowed in the wind
and the storms that arise
without sight
Put thine hand in mine
and by my will it
will all come right

Wanti Wanti
Jamaican Patois

Wanti wanti
but yuh nah
getty getty